A Private Audience

Poems by Beverly Rycroft

THE DRYAD PRESS LIVING POETS SERIES

People! Read Poetry

A Private Audience

First published in Cape Town, South Africa by Dryad Press (Pty) Ltd in 2017
www.dryadpress.co.za

ISBN: 978-0-620-76486-5

First edition, first printing, August 2017

Cover artwork by Ben Grib

DTP and design by Stephen Symons

Printed and bound by Tandym Print (Pty) Ltd

For my father, Earle Holm Graven, 1931–2008

Contents

Section I

We look at the world once, in childhood.
The rest is memory
– Louise Glück

In the beginning

Shaggy and blind,
waves lumber across sand
to sniff bare knees.

Pinned to blue above,
a kingfisher stammers
at its deaf shadow.

Drenched shingle mirrors
clouds, spun dark as fungus
from week-old bread.

Labour

1931. Epidurals
were unheard of
in the Eastern Cape.

Xhosa women rolled
mattresses onto mud-floor
huts, squatted and wept.

My Grandmother had a bed,
and a doctor who tutted
German and Irish.

No good will come of this,
allowing her hand
to grip his, as if to tether

the cord between
a pitching boat
and the quay.

Truth

There was a party
and the grown-ups
sat on the stoep
and drank whisky
and gin. We played
hide-and-seek.
You chased me, I ran
down the steps
and crushed a glass
under my bare foot.

In the car, a tidemark
of blood soaked through
the tight white bandage
our mother wrapped.
From the front seat
you whispered,
Sister, the doctors
will fix you soon.

But the splinter
had already entered
my tiny capillaries,
borne against the
current to lodge like
a stick in the left
chamber of my heart.

Homeland

Goodbye goodbye the children
would whimper, small
and half-asleep as we slotted them
into the combi's waiting alcoves,
the last, most important luggage
of our holiday.

Goodbye goodbye
the cottage exhaled us,
wisps of our voices trailing after
like blonde hairs abandoned
on a new school uniform.

Victrola

My mother's heart is dark
with longing, a black disc
spinning for her children
and their children,
and their children's children,
and also the children of others
(in that strict playing order).

Beneath the hiss and cough
of a thousand scars,
my mother's heart keeps time
with waltz of wind
through oleanders,
rough tango between
Atlantic and rocky shore.

When my daughter climbs up
to lay her head on my mother's
chest, she springs the lid
to a secret cabinet. A needle
drops to the shining hoop and sounds
my childhood bossa nova.

Spells

Whoever was On
kept her back turned,
the rest of us ran
away. She'd shout
K-I-N-G spells
king! then spin
to catch us out.
If you were the one
she caught moving,
you were out of the game.
And so it went,
we were whittled down.
Last girl standing won.

The mammo machine flares,
shackled sun.
My body's trapped,
but my mind's flown
forty years past,
to abandon me
in a yard at dusk.
Behind me
someone waits.
Lift your right arm,
says the radiographer,
lower the left. Keep your body
still. Breathe in.
K-I-N...

Mlungu

I've heard it means
white devils from the sea.
That it comes from the yellow
scum of waves smashed
against the Wild Coast rocks.

In and out of the mirrors
of my home my white face sails,
searching for solid ground.
My cargo of northern vowels
drifts, fractured into new sounds.

The eye of the storm

Winter. Dusk. A boy thumps
at the off-pitch keys
of a Steiner in
a darkened dining room.

In from the verandah
his sisters swoop – bats
ripped from their perches
by a hurricane.

Now the sour white teeth
of the piano have gripped
the boy's fingers and
won't let go. The tune

does as it pleases with
these innocent girls. Points
their grubby toes, whirls them,
thudding, round the silent furniture.

Mother, sentinel,
in the dark doorway
unknowing. I can't tell
where we are headed.
How this story
will end.

The Raft of the Medusa
– a painting by Théodore Géricault

At fifty-six I know
– better than I did
at twenty-three –
how desperation can widen
in a whiplash.
How it can thicken
from trickle to ocean,
leave you clinging
to the raft of your own
splintered body.

At twenty-three,
I stood in front
of that vast canvas
at the Louvre
and flinched.

I knew little, then,
of wreckage or decay.
I gazed at that painting
and could not look away,
while the future considered me
from across the marble floor.

Xhosa lessons

Palate and tongue
my mortar and pestle.
English lips shift
to tut *C C C,*
and clickety-click of X.

Tongue pounds *Q*
like whale threshing tail,
or fat raindrops exploding
in bucket made of tin,

Qô Qô Qô.
Knock on wood.
Let me in.

Squeakers

Pouched like gonads,
the squeakers' hairy crops
prop up the heads
of old hags, as if they've
got it all wrong –
the birth-to-death order.

They start with that creaking,
senile nag, then age rapidly
into youth, shedding their
baldness, their ragged crops
finally swamped by purple,
shimmering lakes that gurgle
as if a stone's been chucked in.

As if that stone's a magnet,
pulsing coordinates for food,
or shelter. Or whatever it is
that lures birds out of thin air
and winds them home again.

No

Between us now a wall of ice.
Layer upon layer of white,
hardened to a gripless blue

that soars above
the flame of your
puny blow-torch tongue.

Too late. Hell's frozen over.
In this wall's translucence, stilled,
a pick-axe, glove and shoe –

cold fossils of your aborted
expeditions, your failure
to hack through.

Foreigner

Unlike these scabbed
city hoboes, my father's pigeons
were of royal blood;
eugenic athletes bred
to find their way home
unerringly, exile after
far-flung exile.

Saturday afternoons,
the phone would herald
their approach. Lookouts
from Queenstown, Grahamstown,
Komga and Hotazel:
Has your dad got a bird yet?

That was our cue:
grab the washing
off the line, call
the dogs inside.
Careful not to slam
the kitchen door.

*Bugger off, the lot
of you,* Dad would yell
after us, hands on hips.
*And don't tie up
the phone,
you bastards.*

Alone in the backyard,
he'd narrow his eyes
at the sky like
ack-ack guns. Straining
to locate the small
suspended mark
the blue would eventually
cough up for him and dangle,
between teasing fingertips:

a bird

swivelling and soaring
in casual victory laps –
once, twice,
above the loft.

One hundred square metres
of fiefdom and King Lear
raging below. Rattling
mealies in a tin, whistling
his special whistle.
Then that old, maddened fury
when the bird
hesitated or dawdled,
or perched coquettishly
in a tree mere metres
from the loft.

Nobody, Mom would sigh
from the kitchen window,
can whistle and swear
at the same time.
Can they?

All our yesterdays.
We could play every part
back then, switch roles
at a moment's notice.
Silence and servility.
Wit or defiance,
and the pain of banishment.
There was a time
I could perform
to a T the whistles
and expletives used
to call the birds in.

Cordelia, Ophelia, Hamlet or Puck.
There are still nights I dream
of Olympian, shimmering-throated
birds. They fly in from
foreign cities to peck at the windows
of empty houses, and peck
in the feeders of abandoned lofts.

The wonderful, magic fortune-telling fish

He caught a fish on Christmas Day
and brought it to my house to say
what he could not, of love. And hate.

A bluefish on a metal plate:
wild dorsals needled, stinking salt,
tail curled up as if it felt

the wind and currents between us.
It cast me back to Xmases past
of heatwaves, ham and paper hats

that bled carmine down our sweating brows.
Where adults spoke through gritted teeth
and crackers spilled miniscule fish

that swam in our sticky palms
and told the truth at a table
groaning with lies.

I fried that fish, chewed his intent
(a dredge of flour, pinch of salt).
I teased flesh from the lethal bones

and ate till just the bones were left –
a carcass picked clean of love.
I know what that fish meant.

After fifty years God breaks His silence

I never promised you
this muggy spring day.
I never promised veld flowers
on Rondebosch Common,
or the whim that makes you
trek towards them, your heart
jolting against the railing
of your ribs like a helium balloon
pleading to be set free.

Each morning, these vygies
are trip-switched open by the sun
to fling hot constellations back
at the sky's icy galaxies.

Just between you and Me.
One small flower more or less
never made much difference
to the rest.

As for your liquid little heart?
It's primed to open and shut
as spring and I decree –
a daisy
an eclipse
a whirring fly.

Spring tide

We knew about the schools
of mullet the mad waves
hurled into the tidal pool.
Also rock cod and bluefish
and even some unidentified
small fry that nibbled
at Ma's toes as she kicked
back after her swim one day.
This made it into
the *Daily Dispatch*,
triggering a long debate.
They were piranhas.
They were not piranhas.
(At the time the townships
were burning.)
Once, my brother
released a shark pup there
and had to fish it out again
when old ladies with flowery
bathing caps complained
like they'd complained
about black children
in the paddling pool.
The waves fumed at the wall
and heaved over sand sharks
and lobsters, bottom feeders
and crabs, stacking them
like planes in a holding pattern,
though in the end I opted
for the open sea and pulled
even freestyle strokes,
above the lot of them.

Section II

We have art that we may not perish of the truth
– Friedrich Nietzsche

Minotaur

He built the labyrinth himself.
Brick by ancient brick.

At night you'd hear
them clicking and stacking
in echoing counterpoint
to the rumble of his curses.

He learned to slather
cement and stone
with brilliant carelessness,
hurl down solid walls
of rage, so skilfully
they'd last a lifetime.
So devious, even
he couldn't find
his way out.

Children?
They were foreign to him.
Medals of his desire,
epaulettes of power.

It's not true what they said
about him devouring them.
He merely threatened to.
And they believed him.

You'll be a man, my son!
– from "If" by Rudyard Kipling

We kept a healthy distance
when Dad took to the rocks,
shouldering his fishing rod,
swinging a bucket of red-bait
or stinking prawns.

If he should slip and fall!
Jesus Christ call your mother
tell her to come quick I've
broken my back. I'm dying.
Fetch your mother fast.

In the kitchen, Ma
would loosen her apron
unhurriedly. Three times
she'd fold that apron up
before stepping onto
the cottage lawn to check
the old man was back
on his feet, whistling
as he cast out again.

He'd only glance back
once to make sure
she was there. She
who kept in her large
hands the nylon line,
the crazy, burning reel,
that stopped the rest of us
from spinning out to sea.

Dynasty

In that house,
furniture seeded itself
across wooden floors.
Clothes ripened and bloomed
in the cupboards upstairs.

Twist of a wrist,
water hissed.
Steel gullets flared
silver tongues.

From the kitchen,
suspended like bats,
the carving knives howled
at the open door:
Where are you going?
When will you be home again?

Nothing in common

Though Mom said it first,
Dad tended to agree.

Still – he added –
after fifty years
of marriage, we have
one thing in common:
Me.

Matchless

My dad was a motorbike champ.
He rammed the pedal
of that 1957 Matchless
with the ball of his foot
and pulled a trigger,
bulleting right to the record-
breaking bend of the East London
track, the trembling chequered flag.
Goggled, gloved, greased-back,
he showed them all –
once and for all.

Even thirty years later
he knew how to dismantle
an engine to its impartial
pieces, pick it apart
until the entire disassembled
beast lay silenced
on his garage floor.
Then reconstruct it,
better than before.

The three of us he dissected too,
laying our soft sections out
in careful rows. No challenge, that.
One skilfully twisted phrase
shattered everything. It was
the putting together again
that baffled him.

Nitrogen deficiency

"I wrote the thesis on it.
And I can tell you now:
it's a sin not to grow
watermelons in this soil.
CO_2, NO_2, 2:3:2.
Look at this leaf.
Then we water them.
If the irrigation doesn't work
your mother'll carry
buckets of water
from the river.
Go on. She loves it.
Wouldn't have it
any other way.

This pink snow, these ticking
black seeds. Have you ever
tasted watermelon like this?
Taste. Now listen:
I'm your father. If I don't
tell you, nobody will.
No man will ever
marry you. Even
your friends don't like you.
Taste. How sweet is that?
I'm only telling you
because I care.

And you are the one
I want to see now,
now I'm dying,
though I still can't

say the word.
Come see me my daughter,
my darling, not a good wife,
not a good mother.
Taste. Taste. Taste."

Nursery Stories

I

Babysitter

A suitcase of nappies
and a vial of morphine.
Dad is delivered
to spend the morning
with me.

II

The enemy of good art.

In my hallway:
three prams
and a Zimmer frame.

III

Rhymes

Water
Daughter
Laughter

What's it like outside?

Partly sunny.
A strong southeaster.
Clouds that shuffle
towards Table Mountain
like pensioners
at a communion rail.

Beside the traffic lights
on Kromboom and Main
a preacher's tie
rears like a viper
in the wind.

He tucks a Bible under
his arm and mutters
over the bent head
of a bergie. God
is with them, God
is in control.
The Man Upstairs
has a plan for all of us.

In the frail-care centre
at Century City
my father dissolves
between Disprin-white sheets

and I heard an astronaut
on the radio say
he saw the blue earth
from two hundred miles
away, and it crackled
with lightning, and he wept.

The Age of Innocence

was showing on TV
and Winona Ryder had just
begun to see: there was
something funny going on
between Daniel Day-Lewis
(her fiancé) and
Michelle Pfeiffer.

In a magnificent garden
where fountains sprinkled
sun, Winona stood
in her white dress,
wondering.

I got up and went
to the bedroom.
I couldn't tell if he was
breathing, lying like
he'd been dumped there.
It was February,
he was naked except
for a nappy, saving us
from more laundry.

I stared down at him, twisted up
in those woman-washed sheets,
recalling how he'd once
vaulted over garden gates
and broken down brick walls.
How he'd mended punctures
and pigeons maimed by wire,

and how I'd believed
– for far too long –
there was nothing
my father could not fix.

Ceasefire

The daughter waits
by the father's bed.
(The bed he still
insists on sharing
with her reluctant
mother each night).

The father lies
keeled into a roll
of cold and heavy
saltiness,
like a torpedoed
battleship.

For decades
they've kept score.
At times, they've each
switched flags
out of mischief
or spite

or the simple delight
of raising a laugh.
She'll be the last
to surrender. Him, his
futile body, the flotsam
and jetsam of love.

Nothing ever happened in King William's Town

Some nights, when this city
won't let me sleep,
I like to remember how
I once squeezed a trigger
and launched a Coke tin
into the humid air.
First shot.

Scene: backyard
of our house in Albert Road.
Dad, Basil the bank manager,
the Coke tin. A pellet gun.
I enter and ask to have a go.
Dad says, *Pull yourself together*
Basil, man. This
is no laughing matter.

As I reach for the rifle
Dad always says, *Listen. Basil.*
Don't give her the gun
before you set the target up.
That daughter of mine
has a very strange
sense of humour.

Witnesses

The sofa crouched
to catch the great weight
as he toppled over,
a rogue elephant darted
at last. On their smooth
white navels, dishes bore
food that was touched
and turned away again.

The carpet crept nearer
to bolster the slurring steps.
The bed held the captured
breath that slowed to the pace
of a legal testament,
the ant-slim weight
of a witnessed signature.

What of the bathroom
that still weeps?
The bath that cannot forget.
Not with Handy Andy
or Chemiclean
can it be scoured
of its voracious memory:
the locked door,
the impartial knives,
the perfect and willing red.

I Spy

Morphine in legal doses.
A fresh delusion each day.
This morning, it's a woman
in halter neck and shorts
parading past the door
of Dad's room.
She's speaking German.
But my father is onto her.
He speaks German, too.

Do you know who
I am? I ask, not
German, not Irish, not
sure of anything
any more.

Dad beckons
me closer.
He whispers:

You
are my daughter.

And I know how to
spell your name.

Action replay

Using just a remote
we can reverse time.
Saturday's rugby match,
for example.

The ball leaps
from the fly half's clutch
as he sprints backwards,
toe–heel, toe–heel,
while the air shrugs
his arced opponent off.

With this device I might
yank you from your bed
to stagger backwards
in a Zimmer frame, shedding
your tartan dressing gown.

One–two, one–two,
I could drive you
suited and tied,
swift reverse-stride,
out of the frail-care front door.

Quick, quick, I could speed
things ten times ten
to a farm, a hot day,
a man on a quad bike
browsing the summer fields.

Watch

Morning after morning
he wakes in frail care,
black watch strapped
to his wrist like a tourniquet.

A wasted finger
raps at the dial. *Where is
your mother, what is
the plan today, when can
I get out of here?*

White sheets, white walls,
white waiting, waiting,
ticking down.
My own breath
stops when he
unclips the strap,
and hands it to me
like a diver, poised
to knife the dark water.

Goodbye

he said,
that most critical
of words.

Then shocking us
with his old grin,
he looped his
giant hand up
like a director,
dropped it suddenly
and shouted

Cut!

Man overboard

Like an astronaut spooled
from his capsule,
you and I are finally parted.

I'm no longer bound
to the phone you operated,
firing commands

Come quickly
I'm dying
It's time now.

Dearest.
At last you're free
to wink in orbit
around my steadied sleep.

Section III

Words, after speech, reach
Into the silence
– Emily Dickinson

Breaking ground

Make us a home there, Dad.
Pace a clearing and hem it off.
Chop down trees, saw wood,
hurl bricks and cement.
Shout for us through
the wide-mouthed windows.

Make us a home there, Dad.
Raise workshops for wood,
lofts for pigeons, greenhouses
and herb distilleries. Plant fields
of watermelon and spanspek.

Wait for us at the top
of the long driveway
in your carpenter's apron
and denim shorts.
When our car finally noses
through the open gates, yell
Where the hell have you been?
and *I'm surprised you bastards*
even bothered to come home.
Then stand in the sun
and sip tea, cooled in the saucer
of an old, chipped cup.

All the houses you built
with such dedication
and rage. Waiting
was never your strongest
trait. We'll keep searching
for you Dad, I swear. Down

by the workshop, up
at the loft. Or on the sofa
in the cool corner of the TV room,
the *Sunday Times* lifting
and falling gently over your face.

A matter of time

In my lounge sits
a facsimile
of my dead father.

In the armchair
Dad always favoured
his brother reclines,
ankle on opposite knee.
That old, familial pose.

With the same
drawling accent
(Dad's voice tracing
a grey scribble behind),
my uncle tells how
once he was left
clinging to the roof
when his wife
took the ladder away.

How long did you hang there, Uncle Pete?

Till my arms got tired, hey.

Arrivals

What if heaven's like
Cape Town International?
Coming out of customs, Dad's
waiting at the barricades
(A miracle! He caught a flight!),
yelling *Where the hell have you been?*
stabbing a finger at his watch
because the red bakkie's parked
in a loading zone. Beside him,
his mother, still on crutches,
though no longer in pain.
She catches my eye and waves,
weeping quietly, while beside her,
Pa Els, her second husband,
and Walter, her first…

No. Too complicated.
Let's just stick with
the scraps of heaven down
here. Like this businessman
off the flight from Brazzaville.
Dropping his briefcase
to the floor, he crouches
to fling his arms wide,
braced for someone
calling from the crowd.

Her little life

I

Sleep

Her skin's a warped mirror,
her mouth a darted seam,
puckered by a foreign hand.

II

Awake

The black dog
brings her home
in his hot jaws
like a treasured bone.

Despair

Less a black dog than a parrot.
You hear its corduroy-ripping
wings long before you spot
its psychedelic whirr,
amplifying as it approaches.

It grapples in rat-cold claws
your scapula or extended arm,
as you hurry across a parking lot
or wave artlessly at a friend.
Everything was okay till now.

Out of the dark it hunches,
green, yellow, traffic-light red,
hopping from shoulder to arm
as if they're limbs of a tree
or a broken-down fence.

Poetry. To pinion
the bird. It sharpens its beak
on the artery in your throat,
twists its gaudy neck to spit
your own husked words back at you.

Kafka's cat
- Kafka kept a sign above his desk that read "Wait"

She waits, patient
as this blank page.
Weary as the infinite
lines tattooing
its bone-white back.

Thoughts glide and flip,
glide back again.
Soft-finned topaz,
gills beetle-brown,
drenched chrome, magnified.

Immobile, tensed,
only her obsidian eyes
skim across, then twitch
and return, like the carriage
of an old typewriter. Patience.

Claw flash. Mercury
Ker-splish!
A muscled thrash
of meaning thuds
to the white page.

The lines bow back
like ring ropes.

Sleight of hand

While she washed dishes
she wondered where they'd gone,
the slicers of bread, the smearers
of jam on counters. The crumblers
of rusks and abandoners
of apple cores.

She supposed they either worked
or slept or watched TV,
or at that very moment stepped
off planes into loud, cold cities,
their last cries fading, transient
as a thunderstorm.

Words splatter like magic
onto her trembling phone:
Love you lots. Chat soon.
She ignores them all,
ladles water over a china plate,
rinsing it like a newborn.

I'm

fixed fast, your Statue of Liberty,
hollowed into corridors
for you to race through.
Lights swarm at each window.
I'm anxious as ants, peering
as meerkats do. Persistent
as a cinema usher, torch probing
for your face, O little stowaway,
out at sea.

Larger than love and fucked-up
as family. Older than
a black-and-white movie.
Crumple-shadowed,
patient as cement.
Numbered, like three hundred
and fifty-four steps.
You'll climb each one,
to my heart, then head.
My crown lights up.
Come home.

Letter to the other side

Here is the news, Dad.
Promise you won't be cross.
In my dreams you still prowl.
Sometimes I stand behind you
till you turn and stamp
your foot and bellow *No!*
in astonishment and joy.

Mom has traded in your Kompressor
for a Mercedes 6.5 and travelled
to America. Twice.
When the electricity fails,
Paul from downstairs
brings tea made on his gas stove.
Sometimes they talk about you.

Every day she goes to sculpture
or art, or tape aids for the blind,
building and shaping those statues
stopped inside her for fifty years,
quietly soaping them down,
closing large fingers around their palms,
rubbing chilly hands to life again.

Sounding the depth

I want to take you for a day
on the water, my brother said.
I will not talk about business
or family. I will load your paintbox
and make a dry seat for you
at one end of my boat while I,
I will fish from the other.

Well, the mountains curled
into womanly lines and the ocean
lay down and let us sail her.
I painted a picture and my
brother cast and reeled and talked
about business and family.

And I touched blue and I touched
green. I touched one brilliant
horizontal yellow and I sank
anchor below the oily surface
of the sea, down to the sand bed
where cast-off rudders rusted,
wordlessly.

Not Adriane

I never forgave you for Paxos.
That holiday, you ignored
my warnings of a taxi strike
and launched us into a maze.
Bribery and back alleyways,
till we finally escaped
from the island and flew home.

But we are old now
and you kept your
promise to marry me.
Old past other pairings,
like the last two pieces
of a cutlery set, jumbled
in a kitchen drawer.

Our passports lie filed
side by side these days.
Nights, I still listen
for a scrap of traffic to fatten
into your car's sound.
Sunday afternoons, like old people,
we nap. Your hand on my hip.
Even in sleep you're steering me.

In the potter's studio

Two rooms away my friends are sighing
over displays of white pitchers and plates.
I've escaped to this bench to yield
what my body wants: a private audience.

Here, bowls fragile as nautilus
have been set afloat on shelves.
Pale-green pods teem with shadows
skimmed from the oak tree outside.

Like a valley cupped to keep water,
all my courage rests in these
hollowed bones. So many questions.
Such kind voices sounding
my name.

End Notes

Page 18:   Baby racing pigeons are called squeakers.

Page 23:   Fortune–telling fish are Christmas-cracker favours in the shape of tiny fish made of cellophane. Placed in the palm of the hand, it is claimed the fish's movements will reveal the holder's true personality.

Acknowledgements

Thanks are due to the editors of the following magazines, in which some of these poems, or versions of them, appeared: *Carapace, New Contrast, New Coin, The Sol Plaatjie Anthology 2011, The Big Issue.* Also to Naomi Jaffa, Michael Laskey and Dean Parkin of the UK Poetry Trust 2014 who assisted in the publication of my chapbook *Calling From the Crowd*, published by the UK Poetry Trust in 2014. I am indebted to them all.

For invaluable commentary on this collection, I wish to thank Robert Berold, Ingrid de Kok, Finuala Dowling, Gus Ferguson and Jackie Kay.

My thanks to Michèle Betty and Joan Hambidge of Dryad Press and to Megan Hall for their meticulous editing and observations.